Pebble™

Character Values
I Am
Generous
by Sarah L. Schuette

Consulting Editor: Gail Saunders-Smith, PhD
Consultant: Madonna Murphy, PhD
Professor of Education, University of St. Francis, Joliet, Illinois
Author, *Character Education in America's Blue Ribbon Schools*

Capstone
press

Mankato, Minnesota

Pebble Books are published by Capstone Press
151 Good Counsel Drive, P.O. Box 669, Mankato, Minnesota 56002
www.capstonepress.com

1 2 3 4 5 6 09 08 07 06 05 04

Library of Congress Cataloging-in-Publication Data
Schuette, Sarah L., 1976–
    I am generous / by Sarah L. Schuette.
    p. cm.—(Character values)
    Includes bibliographical references (p. 23) and index.
    ISBN 0-7368-2570-3 (hardcover)
    1. Generosity—Juvenile literature. [1. Generosity.] I. Title. II. Series.
BJ1533.G4S38 2005
179′.9—dc22   2003024149

Summary: Simple text and photographs illustrate how children can be generous.

Note to Parents and Teachers

The Character Values series supports national social studies
standards for units on individual development and identity.
This book describes generosity and illustrates ways students
can be generous. The photographs support early readers in
understanding the text. The repetition of words and phrases helps
early readers learn new words. This book also introduces early
readers to subject-specific vocabulary words, which are defined in
the Glossary. Early readers may need assistance to read some words
and to use the Table of Contents, Glossary, Read More, Internet
Sites, and Index/Word List sections of the book.

Table of Contents

4

Being Generous

I am generous. I share my time, talents, and books with others.

At Home and School

I am generous at home. I make gifts for my family.

I give the last piece
of pizza to my sister.

I help my friend
study for a test.

I am generous at school. I put away art supplies for my teacher.

In the Community

I share my talents with others. I sing songs.

16

I help my father collect
food for a shelter.

I help my neighbor
shovel snow.

I feel good when I give to others. I am generous.

Glossary

generous—being giving; people who are generous share freely; they give without expecting to get something in return.

neighbor—a person who lives nearby

shelter—a place where people who do not have homes can stay; shelters offer people food to eat and a place to sleep; people often give food to shelters.

study—to spend time learning a subject by reading about it or by practicing it

supplies—materials needed to do something; art supplies include paint, crayons, markers, and paper.

talent—a natural ability or skill; talents are things that people do well.

Read More

Amos, Janine. *Sharing.* Courteous Kids. Milwaukee: Gareth Stevens Publishing, 2002.

Leaney, Cindy. *Field Trip: A Story About Sharing.* Hero Club Character. Vero Beach, Fla.: Rourke, 2004.

Raatma, Lucia. *Generosity.* Character Education. Mankato, Minn.: Bridgestone Books, 2003.

Internet Sites

FactHound offers a safe, fun way to find Internet sites related to this book. All of the sites on FactHound have been researched by our staff.

Here's how:

1. Visit *www.facthound.com*
2. Type in this special code **0736825703** for age-appropriate sites. Or enter a search word related to this book for a more general search.
3. Click on the **Fetch It** button.

FactHound will fetch the best sites for you!

Index/Word List

Word Count: 89
Early-Intervention Level: 9

Editorial Credits
Mari C. Schuh, editor; Jennifer Bergstrom, series designer and illustrator;
  Enoch Peterson, book designer; Karen Hieb, product planning editor

Photo Credits
Capstone Press/Gem Photo Studio/Dan Delaney, all

The author dedicates this book in memory of her aunt Evelyn Woestehoff,
  of Belle Plaine, Minnesota.